Unity and the
FLAME OF LOVE

Unity and the FLAME OF LOVE

Deacon Norman Alexander

www.DeaconNormanAlexander.com

UNITY AND THE FLAME OF LOVE
Deacon Norman Alexander

Copyright 2019, Deacon Norman Alexander

No part of this book may be reproduced, stored in a retrieval system, or transmitted by any means, electronic, mechanical, photocopying, recording, or otherwise, without written permission from the author.

Editor: Sam Severn
Graphic Designer: Debbi Stocco, MyBookDesigner.com

Scripture quotations are from the New American Bible and the Douay Rheims Bible.

paperback ISBN 13: 978-0-9912011-9-8
hardback ISBN 13: 978-0-9912011-7-4
ebook ISBN 13: 978-0-9912011-8-1

For information regarding permission, write to:
Permissions Department
6102 Explorer Ave
Bartlett, TN 38134

Or contact via website:
www.deaconnormanalexander.com

Table of Contents

Introduction 9

Chapter 1. Adam — Son of God 13
    The Drought 14
    The Body 14
    The Interior 14
    The Head 15
    The Fall 16
    Redemption 16

Chapter 2: Israel — Firstborn Son of God 19
    The Drought 20
    The Fall 21
    Drought Predicted by Elijah 22
    Interior 23
    The Choice to Believe or Not 24
    Elijah and the Prophets of Baal 25
    The Drought Continues 26
    The Body 26
    Interior 27
    The Choice to Believe or Not 28

Chapter 3: Jesus Christ — The Only Begotten Son of God 31
    Drought 32
    The Body 33
    Interior: John 6 — Multiplication of the Loaves 35
    Head: Choice to Believe or Not 36
    Salvation 37
    Jesus Predicts the End of the Drought 39
    The Body 40

 The Interior 41
 Choice—To Believe or Not to Believe 42

Chapter 4: Twelve Apostles—Firstborn of Jesus 45
 Head: Falling into Ruin 46
 Interior 48
 Body 49
 Choice to Believe or Not Believe 50

Chapter 5: Twelve Franciscan Friars—Firstborn of Jesus ... 51
 The Body 52
 The Interior 53
 The Head 54
 The Face 55
 Confessions of St. Augustine:
  Chapter 12 - The Voice in the Garden 56

Chapter 6: The Twelve Priests of Hungary—Firstborn of Jesus 59
 The Drought 60
 The Body 61
 Interior 63
 The Head 63
 The Face 64

Summary 67
 The Marian Fathers of the Immaculate Conception of the Blessed
  Virgin Mary 68
 Missionaries of Charity 69

Elizabeth Kindelmann: The sweet Redeemer asked me to pray with Him the prayer that expresses His deepest desires:

May our feet journey together.

May our hands gather in unity.

May our hearts beat in unison.

May our souls be in harmony.

May our thoughts be as one.

May our ears listen to the silence together.

May our glances profoundly penetrate each other.

May our lips pray together to gain mercy from the Eternal Father.

Jesus: "This prayer is an instrument in your hands. By collaborating with Me, Satan will be blinded by it, and because of his blindness, souls will not be led into sin."

Introduction

THE PRAYER THAT JESUS GAVE to Elizabeth Kindelmann is like a book. It is also like poetry that can be read from top to bottom or in reverse order. Jesus revealed to Elizabeth why some things in her younger days did not work out: because He did not allow them to. Jesus was saving her for the special mission of *The Flame of Love of the Immaculate Heart of Mary*. Everything that she failed to accomplish was later accomplished on a grander scale, and the level of Elizabeth Kindelmann's success cannot be measured.

Though the prayer itself may seem to have nothing to do with Elizabeth, the story always leads back to her life and experiences. The creation of the first man is written in this prayer. The efforts of Elijah to bring the Israelites back to their senses, and of our Lord Jesus, who came for the lost sheep of the house of Israel, are hidden in this prayer. Even the history of Christianity is affected by this prayer, which has earned the title, "Unity Prayer." The name is very fitting—unity is what it accomplishes. Most obviously, the union is between Jesus and

Elizabeth Kindelmann. It is a mystical union, and those willing to follow in her footsteps are also invited to experience this mystical union. The prayer reveals a story much larger than life, and it expands over salvation history.

The primary motivation for writing about this prayer is to encourage *Flame of Love* devotees to look deeper into the mysteries of the *Flame of Love* devotion. We have been invited to contemplate the mysteries of the Kingdom, and Jesus wants to enlighten us with the Flame of Love from the Immaculate Heart of His and our Blessed Mother.

There were a few things Elizabeth Kindelmann was not able to accomplish in her youth. A list of things she aspired to accomplished but was not privileged to experience includes:

1. Elizabeth wanted to gain an education. She attended elementary school for a short period (approximately four years) but did not have the money to pay for the exams.
2. She wanted to join the Sisters of Perpetual Adoration. She did not have the money needed to contribute for the support of the community or to buy her own clothing.
3. She wanted to become a missionary sister, but was rejected because she was an orphan without a home. The superior said she did not have a true vocation, and Elizabeth only wanted to become a missionary because she was an orphan.
4. Her last attempt to become a missionary sister ended with the prioress of the order telling her Jesus had

another mission for her—a mission she must fulfill to the best of her ability.
5. Even with these would-be failures and rejections, Elizabeth's main interests in life remained gaining an education, making people aware of the Lord, and teaching religion.

The following illustration reveals how Jesus allowed Elizabeth to accomplish what she aspired to. This chart leads into Chapter One and the Creation story, which is reflected in the Unity Prayer. However, it is the Fall of Humanity, and our first parents being cast out of Paradise that highlights the need for unity. The Fall is the beginning of division and tension even within the individual, where spirit and flesh are at war. God has a plan to unite his scattered children and lead them back to Paradise. *The Flame of Love of the Immaculate Heart of Mary* emerges as the fulfillment of the missionary work needed to unite the children of God:

JESUS	Unity Prayer	Elizabeth Kindelmann	Spiritual Diary
REDEEMER	1. May our feet journey together 2. May our hands gather in unity	Missionary	Page 160: Jesus said, "You no longer doubt that I have chosen you to be a worker of Redemption. Many missionary priests cannot do more than you do."
MUSICIAN	3. May our hearts beat in unison 4. May our souls be in harmony	Harp	Page 233: "My Elizabeth, you have become My harp. The sacrifices which you continually accept are the chords of the harp." Page 275: "On the chords of your soul, I play the melody of repentance."
TEACHER	5. May our thoughts be as one 6. May our ears listen to the silence together	Student	Page 83: "I teach you, so you learn and teach others how to gather souls."
ADORED	7. May our glances profoundly penetrate each other 8. May our lips pray together to gain mercy from the Eternal Father	Perpetual Adoration and Intercession	Page 47: "During the day, let not the flame of your sacrifices fade away. See to it that the love of many victim souls rise up to Me, and through My intercession, obtain the mercy of the heavenly Father."

Chapter One

Adam—Son of God

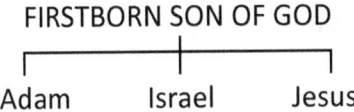

WHEN I THINK OF THE Creation story, I always picture the earth submerged underwater and covered in darkness. This seems accurate when we consider the Word of God in the first chapter of Genesis, which reads, *"In the beginning, when God created the heavens and the earth, the earth was a formless wasteland, and darkness covered the abyss, while a mighty wind swept over the waters"* (Genesis 1:1-2). It appears that the Lord God displaced the darkness with light, and the waters with dry land. The earth became habitable for growing plants, but only after the Lord God freed the earth from being submerged underwater. Once the dry land appeared, God said, *"Let the earth bring forth vegetation: every kind of plant that bears seed and every kind of fruit tree on earth that bears fruit with its seed in it. And so it happened* (Genesis 10:11).

The Drought

Now let's consider the second story of Creation in the second chapter of Genesis. *"At the time when the Lord God made the earth and the heavens – while as yet there was no field shrub on earth and no grass of the field had sprouted, for the Lord God had sent no rain upon the earth and there was no man to till the soil, but a stream was welling up out of the earth and was watering all the surface of the ground – The Lord God formed man out of the clay of the ground and blew into his nostrils the breath of life, and so man became a living being"* (Genesis 2:4-7).

The Body

The appearance of a drought would mean that the dust particles remained separate. Nothing can be built from dust alone, and it would take water to hold the dust particles together in order to form a being, such as man. Made of many particles and formed into a single being—this is how the Lord God chose to form man. This is the first of three important phases of creation when God formed man from the clay of the earth.

The Interior

When God blew the breath of life into the nostrils of the man, life began for him. Man became a living being. We cannot be certain about the body of the first man, Adam, or its properties before he sinned, since there was no corruption or dying. The body of the first man we may presume was somewhat different than our earthly bodies. Man became a living being when he received the breath of life from God. For us, this means we have a soul that animates our body, and a heart that takes the breath of life to every part of the body. Since *The Flame of Love of the Immaculate Heart of Mary* first came forth from Mount Carmel, I believe it is important to reflect on what St. John of the Cross speaks of in his book, *The Dark Night*. St. John speaks of the interior life as a soul with an upper chamber and a lower chamber. The upper chamber is spiritual, and the lower chamber is sensual. We can relate this to the soul as the upper chamber that is purely spiritual, and the heart which is flesh, but reflects our spiritual being.

THE HEAD

Man became a living being, yet he needed something to sustain his life. God gave man the Word of God to sustain his life for all eternity. Had man obeyed the Word of God, he could have avoided death. So, the Word of God came to man through his hearing and must remain alive in order to govern man's body. The head governs the body, because the Word of God governs from above. In these three steps God created man. First the body, then the breath of life causes man to become a living being, and in the third step man was given the Word of God to sustain his life. He had a choice to obey God by eating from all the trees in the garden which God proclaimed were good for food or to disobey God by eating the fruit from the Tree of Knowledge of Good and Evil, which God forbid him to eat from. The choice also was to remain faithful and trust God; to believe

God and obey His Word or to demand proof and certitude, which is what the devil had offered. For man to remain the image and likeness of God, he must remain good. If he chooses good and evil, then he is no longer all good and holy as his Creator. All good is perfect, but good and evil is flawed.

The Fall

God created man and elevated him to an exalted position, giving him dominion over the earth. When man disobeyed God, he rejected the Word of God. The consequences were tragic: the breath of life returned to God, and man returned to the ground from which he was taken. God raised man up from the clay of the earth in three steps. Man fell from grace in three steps. First, he sinned by eating the forbidden fruit. Next, he and his wife covered their loins with fig leaves, and lastly, they hid themselves from God among the trees. These three steps are in reverse order of the Creation.

Redemption

God in His infinite love and mercy gave the man and woman the chance to repent. Since they were not willing to repent, God saved them from eternal damnation by preventing them from eating the fruit from the Tree of Life. God did not want the man and his wife to live forever in an unrepentant state as the fallen angels did. Thus he placed the cherubim with the flaming sword going every way to prevent the man and his wife from eating the fruit from the Tree of Life. This is a great act of mercy. To eat from both trees is damnation; man must choose one or the other. If he reserves the right to eat from the Tree of Knowledge of Good and Evil—which means he judges for himself what is good and evil—he must not eat from the Tree of Life, and live forever in this rebellious state.

The man and woman covered their loins with fig leaves, but God covered their loins with skins or leather garments. Something was sacrificed and gave up the breath in place of Adam and Eve. As far as returning to the ground, they hid themselves from God among the trees. God's answer to this was to cast them out of Paradise facing East. Even this was an act of mercy and part of God's plan of salvation. Yes, they hid among the trees to avoid returning to the ground. God's plan of salvation allows for humankind to be preserved, and life for us begins hidden in the womb. Although humanity was cast out of Paradise, it was with the purpose of bringing them back.

All the descendants of Adam share a common story. This is our story, and probably what Dr. Martin Luther King Jr. meant when he spoke of the universal brotherhood of all mankind. This universal brotherhood consists of everyone who inherits the original sin. All the kingdoms of the world are made up of the descendants of Adam, banished from Paradise when our first parents Adam and Eve were cast out facing East. The kingdoms of the world are scattered throughout the earth as the dust particles were before the Lord God formed the first man from the clay of the ground. The water united the particles of dust into clay, and from this unity of members God formed the body of the first man, Adam. The genealogy of Jesus Christ in the Gospel of Luke descends in chronological order down to the first man, Adam, the son of God.

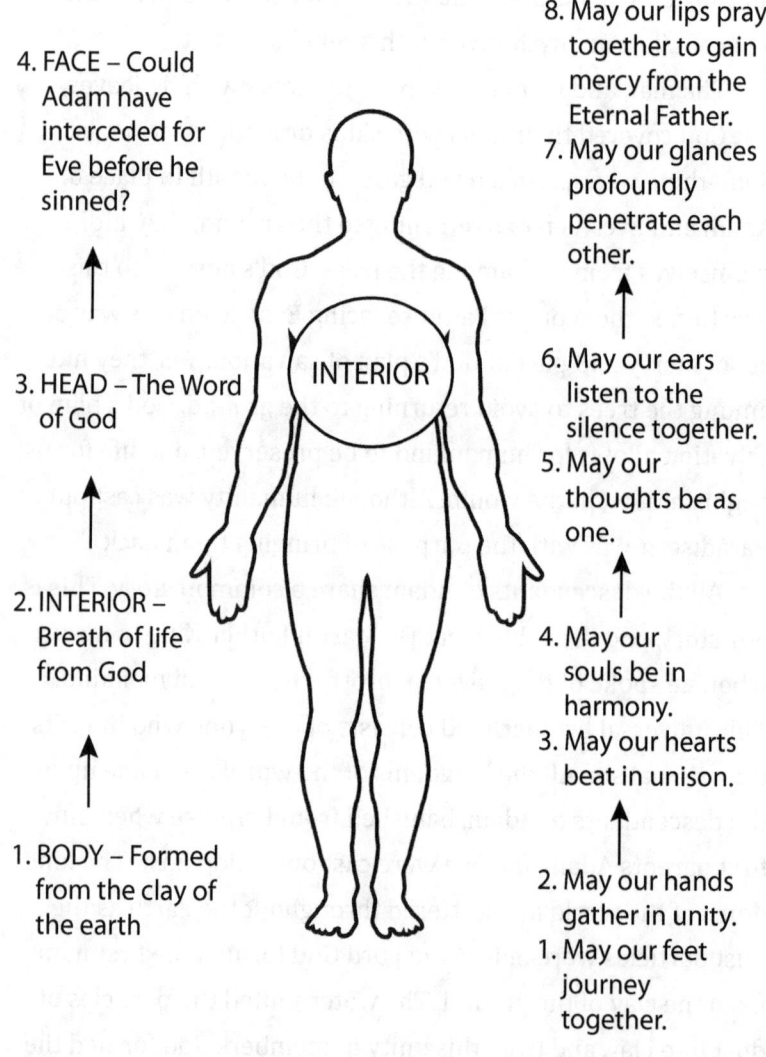

Chapter Two

Israel—Firstborn Son of God

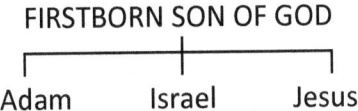

GOD FORMED A PEOPLE FROM among the nations of the world. When it appeared that all of humanity would be lost to the worship of false gods, the Lord began to form a people He would call his own, beginning with Abram and Sarai.

After 430 years of slavery in Egypt, God called His son Israel out of Egypt. The Lord instructed Moses to say to Pharaoh: "*Thus says the Lord: Israel is my son, my first-born. Hence I tell you: Let my son go, that he may serve me. If you refuse to let him go, I warn you, I will kill your son, your first-born*" (Exodus 4:22-23).

The Drought

The tribes of Israel went to Egypt to escape a severe famine that affected the whole world. After 430 years of slavery, Israel faced a famine in the sense that they were not allowed to offer sacrifice to God. However, on the night of the first Passover, the Israelites offered sacrifice to God and were thus permitted by Pharaoh to leave Egypt and go on a three-day journey in the desert to offer sacrifice to God. Coming through the Red Sea was a symbol of baptism, and they were brought together as one body in a similar way as the first man, Adam, was formed from the clay of the ground. Israel came through the Red Sea and were formed into a people, a nation, a kingdom of priests.

Israel became a living being when God began to dwell in their midst. Moses was their prophet, and Aaron their high priest, but they did not have a king, because God is their Savior and their King. The interior life of Israel was that the living God dwelled in their midst. No other nation in the world had the Creator dwelling in their midst. All peoples of the world were worshiping false gods, the worship of creation and creatures.

Why was Israel given this privilege? It appears that God wanted to use them to lead the rest of the world back to Himself, the true God, creator of heaven and earth. God chose them, they did not choose God. Another reason Israel would not have a king is because God wanted to use them to drive out the wicked nations from the land of Canaan. Israel did not have its feet planted among the trees, as Adam attempted to do. A king must have a domain. And Israel did not have a domain. They were serving as God's military to take back what belonged to God, which is the whole world.

THE FALL

The Israelites were allowed many opportunities to be the image and likeness of God, but they continued to put God to the test. Adam fell as prophet, when he disobeyed the Word of God. As priest his sacrifice was not acceptable; they covered their loins with fig leaves. Adam gave up dominion over the earth and became a slave. He was no longer a king, and he could not hide among the trees from God, because Paradise was no longer his domain.

God gave Israel the opportunity to succeed as prophet, priest and King. Moses the prophet disobeyed God when he struck the rock twice, because he was instructed to speak to the rock. Because of this, Moses was not allowed to enter the Promised Land. Aaron the high priest made the golden calf, and the firstborn of Israel lost their place of honor leading the worship. When Israel demanded to have a King, although this was against the Will of God, He let them have their way. However, King Solomon—who built the temple, known as the First Temple—led the Israelites away from the temple worship. The temple was the only place permitted to offer sacrifice, and the sacrifices were to be offered by the Levite priest. Solomon sinned as Adam did, when he listened to his wives and disobeyed God. In reality, Solomon disobeyed God first by marrying foreign women, and afterwards he listened to his wives. All the kings of Israel continued in the sin of Solomon. The sin could not be inherited as the original sin, but the people caused themselves to be banished from the law, the priesthood, and the temple. Every king of Israel after Solomon appointed laymen to offer sacrifice in the high places. This is why I say that the kings of Israel continued in the sin of Solomon. They were banished from the temple. Solomon caused them to be banished from the temple as Adam caused us to be banished from Paradise. The kings of Israel functioned as men do in reproduction—the exception being that the sin is not inherited.

Drought Predicted by Elijah

God does not give up on his people. He sent Elijah to bring them back to their senses, and to turn their hearts back to their fathers. *"Elijah said to Ahab: 'As the Lord, the God of Israel, lives, whom I serve, during these years there shall be no dew or rain except at my word'"* (1 Kings 17:1). The drought was severe and the brook that Elijah drank from ran dry, because no rain had fallen in the land. The Lord said to him: *"Move on to Zarephath of Sidon and stay there. I have designated a widow there to provide for you. He left and went to Zarephath. As he arrived at the entrance of the city, a widow was gathering sticks there; he called out to her, 'Please bring me a small cupful of water to drink'"* (1 Kings 17: 9-10). Elijah used this opportunity to draw her to himself. The cup of water is the symbol of what unites her and her family to Elijah, although what Elijah will give to her is superior to a small cup of water. *"She left to get it, and he called out after her, 'Please bring along a bit of bread.' 'As the Lord, your God, lives,' she answered, 'I have nothing baked;*

there is only a handful of flour in my jar and a little oil in my jug. Just now I was collecting a couple of sticks, to go in and prepare something for myself and my son; when we have eaten it, we shall die.' 'Do not be afraid,' Elijah said to her. 'Go and do as you propose. But first make me a little cake and bring it to me. Then you can prepare something for yourself and your son. For the Lord, the God of Israel, says, "The jar of flour shall not go empty, nor the jug of oil run dry, until the day when the Lord sends rain upon the earth." (1 Kings 17:11-14)." With these words Elijah gave the widow a drink, the Word of God. The widow and her son were united with Elijah as a family.

INTERIOR

"She left and did as Elijah had said. She was able to eat for a year, and he and her son as well; the jar of flour did not go empty, nor the jug of oil run dry, as the Lord had foretold through Elijah" (1 Kings 17:15-16). She experienced an interior resurrection since she was at the point of death, but now lives because she believed the Word of God. Yet, it appears that they had not reached the highest level in their ascent to Mount Carmel.

"Some time later her son grew sick and died. So she said to Elijah, 'Why have you done this to me. O man of God? Have you come to me to call attention to my guilt and to kill my son?'" (1 Kings 17:18) It is interesting to note that some Bible translations, especially earlier ones, read: *call attention to my sin.* Not sins, but sin in the singular sense. Again, this is a reference to St. John of the Cross and *The Dark Night.*

"Give me your son," Elijah said to her. Taking him from her lap, he carried him to the upper room where he was staying, and laid him on his own bed. He called out to the Lord: 'O Lord my God, will you afflict even the widow with whom I am staying by killing her son?' Then he stretched himself out upon the child three times and called out to the Lord: 'O Lord, my God, let the life breath return to the body of this child.' The Lord heard the prayer of Elijah; the life breath returned to the child's body and he revived. Taking the child, Elijah brought him down into the house from the upper room and gave him to his mother. 'See!' Elijah said to her, 'your son is alive.'"

THE CHOICE TO BELIEVE OR NOT

"Now indeed I know that you are a man of God," the woman replied to Elijah. "The word of the Lord comes truly from your mouth" (1 Kings 17:19-24). Her son was raised to life and she believed, but it was because she was able to see. As Elijah said to her, "See! your son is alive." She was given the choice to believe or not believe and for her, seeing was believing. She put her trust in the Word of the Lord from the mouth of the prophet and she was allowed to see. Faith comes through hearing but the faithful will be allowed to see and understand what they believe by faith. *"The word of the Lord comes truly from your mouth"* is what Eve did not believe about Adam. Our troubles began and continues in the rejection of legitimately established authority.

Elijah and the Prophets of Baal

The story of Elijah and the widow sets the stage for Elijah and the Prophets of Baal. Elijah moved in with the widow and this foreshadows Jesus moving in with the widow Elizabeth Kindelmann. Moreover, Jesus moved in with Elizabeth, John the Baptist's mother. Elizabeth, Zechariah's wife, is not a widow, but her husband lost his voice, the way Adam lost his voice as prophet. If Adam and Eve were married as prophet and prophetess, when Adam sinned, he lost his voice and experienced a spiritual death. The prophetess had become widowed. Jesus restored Zechariah's voice and He would also go and search for Adam in the belly of the earth, in the same way that he freed John the Baptist from the original sin from within his mother's womb. John the Baptist gathered the Israelites the way Elijah gathered the Israelites on Mount Carmel. John the Baptist had to first go out to them, then draw them to himself in baptism, but this was done so that Jesus would baptize them with the Holy Spirit and with fire. *The Flame of Love Prayer* that Jesus gave to Elizabeth Kindelmann allowed her to become a missionary with Jesus. We are called to become missionaries in the same way. May our feet journey together as John the Baptist and Elijah did. May our hands gather in unity to unite families, strengthen the faith of Christians and ultimately help unbelievers to put their trust in God.

The Drought Continues

So how is the story of Elijah and the widow prophetic in revealing the story of Elijah and the Prophets of Baal? When Elijah announced the drought, he also revealed that it would be at his word that the drought would end. The false gods that Israel had put their trust in could not bring rain. Elijah would have to show the Israelites that he is the prophet of the true God of Israel and he could bring the rain because he speaks the Word of the Lord.

"*Long afterward, in the third year, the Lord spoke to Elijah. 'Go, present yourself to Ahab,' he said, 'that I may send rain upon the earth.' Now the famine in Samaria was bitter*" (1 Kings 18:1,2). The grass of the field and the shrubs would not grow although the seeds remained in the ground. In addition, Jezebel had killed all the prophets of the Lord, so only Elijah remained. The Lord heard the blood of Abel crying out to him from the ground. The blood of the prophets during the time of Elijah would more than likely have cried out to the Lord. Even in our time the blood of the martyrs is seed for the Church.

The Body

"Elijah told Ahab, 'Now summon all Israel to me on Mount Carmel, as well as the four hundred and fifty prophets of Baal and the four hundred prophets of Asherah who eat at Jezebel's table. So, Ahab sent to all the Israelites and had the prophets assemble on Mount Carmel.'" This is how Elijah drew all the Israelites to himself. "*Elijah appealed to all the people and said,*

'How long will you straddle the issue? If the Lord is God, follow him; if Baal, follow him.' The people, however, did not answer him. So Elijah said to the people, 'I am the only surviving prophet of the Lord, and there are four hundred and fifty prophets of Baal. Give us two young bulls. Let them choose one, cut it into pieces, and place it on the wood, but start no fire. I shall prepare the other and place it on the wood, but shall start no fire. You shall call on your gods, and I will call on the Lord. The God who answers with fire is God.' All the people answered, 'Agreed'" (1 Kings 18:19-24). The prophets of Baal offered their sacrifice and called on Baal from morning until noon, but no one answered. They slashed themselves with swords and spears, as was their custom, until blood gushed over them. But there was not a sound; no one answered, and no one was listening.

INTERIOR

"Then Elijah said to all the people, 'Come here to me.' When they had done so, he repaired the altar of the Lord which had been destroyed. He took twelve stones, for the number of tribes of the sons of Jacob, to whom the Lord had said, 'Your name shall be Israel.' He built an altar in honor of the Lord with the stones and, made a trench around the altar large enough for two seahs of grain" (1 Kings 18:30-32). Elijah repaired the altar in the way that he restored life to the widow and her son, especially since they were at the point of death when he met them. The two of them ate from the flour and oil which did not run out.

The young bull was cut into pieces and laid on the wood. It is obvious that the bull was dead, but Elijah had water poured on the bull three times as he had stretched himself over the widow's son three times. Four jars of water poured over the holocaust three times and filled the trench. *"At the time for offering sacrifice, the prophet Elijah came forward and said, 'Lord, God of Abraham, Isaac, and Israel, let it be known this day that you are God in Israel and that I am your servant and have done all these things by your command. Answer me, Lord! Answer me, that this people may know that you, Lord, are God and that you have brought them back to their senses.' The Lord's fire came down and consumed the holocaust, wood, stones and dust, and it lapped up the water in the trench."*

THE CHOICE TO BELIEVE OR NOT

"Seeing this, all the people fell prostrate and said, 'The Lord is God! The Lord is God!'" (1 King 18:36-39) The fire of the Lord consumed the sacrifice as the breath of life returned to the widow's son. Likewise, the people believed because they had the opportunity to see. It was proven to them that the Lord is God, and Elijah is his prophet.

ELIJAH AND THE WIDOW		ELIJAH AND ISRAEL	
Body	Elijah and the widow- Bring me a small cup of water	Body	Gather all Israel on Mt. Carmel: Come here to me
Interior	1. Flour and oil 2. Raised her son to life	Interior	1. Repair the altar 2. Fire consumed the sacrifice
Head	Choice Believed—Now I know you are a man of God.	Head	Choice Believed—The Lord is God! The Lord is God!

Chapter Three

Jesus Christ—The Only Begotten Son of God

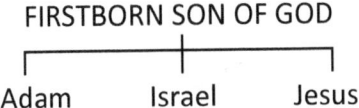

In the beginning was the Word,
and the Word was with God,
and the Word was God.

THE PROLOGUE OF THE GOSPEL of John reveals a new creation unfolding. The opening words make clear that the Creator existed in the beginning. The Word that gives life and sustains life has entered time in order to dwell with humanity. He is the light that came to lead us out of darkness, and free us from the bondage of sin and death. St. Paul explained that the law is slavery, because it brings consciousness of sin. Jesus came to free the Israelites, those born under the law, because He is the New Israel. Jesus came to free all those born of a woman, who inherit the original sin. He is the New Adam.

Jesus entered the world of humanity by becoming one of us. He entered time in order to lead us to eternity with God. The Jews expected Elijah to come before the Messiah. Jesus revealed to his disciples that Elijah had already come, and they did to him whatever they chose. The disciples realized He was talking about John the Baptist. John is the last of a cycle of prophets that began with Elijah. The Catechism of the Catholic Church says that John the Baptist came in the spirit and power of Elijah. God sent Elijah to bring the Israelites to their senses, to unite those scattered and living in the shadow of death and darkness. John the Baptist is the last prophet sent to prepare the way of the Lord, as one crying in the wilderness.

Drought

Whenever the Israelites needed to hear from God, because they had become enslaved by other nations or needed directions from the Lord, they turned to the prophet and priest. If there were no prophet, they waited until a prophet arose to tell them what they must do. For a long period, there was no prophet in Israel, until the birth of John the Baptist. When Judas Maccabee was purifying the temple, he deliberated what ought to be done with the altar of holocausts that had been desecrated. "*The happy thought came to them to tear it down, lest it be a lasting shame to them that the Gentiles had defiled it; so they tore down the altar. They stored the stones in a suitable place on the temple hill, until a prophet should come and decide what to do with them* (Mac 1 4:45-46)." John the Baptist appeared as Elijah to end the drought. "*And the crowds* asked him, 'What then should we do?' He said to them in reply, 'Whoever has two cloaks should share with the person who has none. And whoever has food should do likewise.'" Even tax collectors came to be baptized and they said to him, 'Teacher, what should we do?' He answered them, 'Stop collecting more than what is prescribed.' Soldiers also asked him, 'And what is it that we should do?' He told them, 'Do not practice extortion, do not falsely accuse anyone, and be satisfied with your wages'" (Luke 3:10-14). It appears John spoke prophetic to the soldiers in that the soldiers guarding Jesus' tomb were paid to lie and say that Jesus's disciples came and stole his body after the Resurrection.

John is Elijah and he came to bring the Israelites to their senses. He preached a baptism for the forgiveness of sins, and taught the people to produce good fruits as evidence of their repentance. In order to unite those scattered because of sin, they needed to repent. Moreover, they are united by water. The baptized became a single entity because they became disciples of John. Even so, John's mission was to prepare them to become disciples of Jesus, because Jesus would baptize them with the Holy Spirit and with fire.

The Body

John is a symbol of the one who ended the drought. When he baptized Jesus, the heavens opened up and the Holy Spirit descended on Jesus. In reality, Jesus will end the drought that has lasted since the time of Adam. In the Gospel of John, Jesus used signs to reveal what He is accomplishing in the spiritual kingdom. He came to a town of Samaria called Sychar. "*Jacob's* well was there. Jesus, tired from his journey, sat down there at the well. It was about noon. A woman of Samaria came to draw water. Jesus said to her, 'Give me a drink.' The Samaritan woman said to him, 'How can you, a Jew, ask me, a Samaritan woman, for a drink?' (For Jews use nothing in common with Samaritans.) Jesus answered and said to her, 'If you knew the gift of God and who is saying to you, "Give me a drink," you would have asked him and he would have given you living water'" (John 4:6,7,9,10). Jesus revealed to her, "'Whoever drinks the water I shall give will never thirst; the water I shall give will become in him a spring of water welling up to eternal life'" (John 4:14).

He drew her to himself and told her to go call her husband and come back. She answered, "I do not have a husband." Jesus answered her, "You are right in saying, 'I do not have a husband.' For you have had five husbands, and the one you have now is not your husband. What you have said is true." The woman said to him, "Sir, I can see that you are a prophet" (John 4:17-19). She went to her town and told the people about Jesus and how he told her everything about herself. "Could he possibly be the Messiah?" The people came out of the town to meet Jesus. The Samaritans invited Jesus to stay with them; He stayed there two days. First, they believed the woman, but many more began to believe in Him because of His Word.

The disciples had been urging Jesus to eat, but He said to them, "My food is to do the will of the one who sent me and to finish his work" (John 4:34). Perhaps Jesus wanted to draw the Samaritans to himself because they had been scattered by the Assyrians, who destroyed Israel as a nation in 722 B.C. The Assyrians imported five other nations to live among the Israelites and intermarry with them. Jesus drew them to Himself and united them as believers.

INTERIOR
JOHN 6—MULTIPLICATION OF THE LOAVES

Jesus went across the Sea of Galilee. A large crowd followed Him, because they saw the signs He was performing on the sick. Everyone who followed the signs was led to Jesus. Jesus used this opportunity to repair the altar. The altar must be repaired for the sacrifice to be offered. He had twelve disciples to help distribute the loaves and the fish. It is the image of the twelve tribes of Israel being restored. *"Then Jesus took the loaves, gave thanks, and distributed them to those who were reclining, and also as much of the fish as they wanted. When they had had their fill, he said to his disciples, 'Gather the fragments left over, so that nothing will be wasted.' So they collected them, and filled twelve wicker baskets with fragments from the five barley loaves that had been more than they could eat"* (John 6:11-13). They had been fed by God, as the Israelites were fed manna in the desert. The loaves and the fish multiplied because God is infinite. The scene foreshadows the Eucharistic celebration; even the fragments are not wasted. The source is infinite, and the value is priceless.

Head
Choice to Believe or Not

"When the people saw the sign he had done, they said, 'This is truly the prophet, the one who is to come into the world.' Since Jesus knew that they were going to come and carry him off to make him king, he withdrew again to the mountain alone" (John 6:14-15). The people believed, because they saw for themselves the sign that pointed to Jesus. However, Jesus did not come to be an earthly ruler. He is King of kings of a Kingdom that has no end. It appears they were not ready to comprehend a heavenly Kingdom.

The next day, the crowd saw that neither Jesus nor his disciples were there. They climbed into boats and came to Capernaum looking for Jesus. When they found Him across the sea they said to him, *"Rabbi, when did you get here? Jesus answered them and said, 'Amen, amen, I say to you, you are looking for me not because you saw signs but because you ate the loaves and were filled. Do not work for food that perishes but for the food that endures for eternal life, which the Son of Man will give you'"* (John 6:25-27). For those who lived under the law, the words of Jesus must have been perplexing. The covenant they lived is in the flesh, and Jesus was speaking about a spiritual kingdom. It will take faith to believe in Jesus. They were able to believe that He is the one they were expecting, because He provided what they needed to fill their bellies. Yet, they did not accept His words: *"I am the bread that came down from heaven."* (John 6:41) or, *"For this is the will of my Father, that everyone who sees the Son and believes in him may have eternal life, and I shall raise him on the last day"* (John 6:40). Essentially, they believed in the multiplication of the loaves, but they were not able to believe that Jesus had the power and authority to raise the dead back to life. Jesus continued to reinforce the fact that, *"Whoever eats my flesh and drinks my blood has eternal life, and I will raise him on the last day"* (John 6:54). *Then many of his disciples who were listening said, "This saying is hard; who can accept it?"* (John 6:60)

"As a result of this, many of his disciples returned to their former way of life and no longer accompanied him. Jesus then said to the Twelve, 'Do you also want to leave?' Simon Peter answered him, 'Master, to whom shall we go? You have the words of eternal life. We have come to believe and are convinced that you are the Holy One of God.' Jesus answered them, 'Did I not choose you twelve? Yet is not one of you a devil?' He was referring to Judas, son of Simon the Iscariot; it was he who would betray him, one of the Twelve" (John 6:66-71).

Salvation

God, who is infinitely good and just, has the right to punish—and He does punish when necessary. It may be difficult at times for us to distinguish between mercy and punishment. Sometimes, what appears as punishment is actually mercy. For example, our first parents were prevented from eating from the Tree of Life and cast out of Paradise. Many of the saints have helped us to understand suffering as a means of reparation, and Purgatory as purification for our souls. The most important aspect of the mystery of suffering is that suffering does not change God.

Sometimes humans desire to see the perpetrators of violent crimes suffer punishment. We all agree that these criminals should be removed from society for the safety of law-abiding citizens. Yet, it is debatable whether seeing someone suffer promotes healing to those offended. While we may sometimes feel that justice has been served to witness the execution of an offender, it is difficult if not impossible to determine how this helps to purify the soul of the person witnessing the execution.

The Crucifixion of our Lord and Savior Jesus Christ is the greatest mystery of suffering, and we may not fully understand until we see God face-to-face. Some things are revealed to us, and we should meditate on the mysteries of the Passion. We are taught that Jesus paid the price for our salvation. He reconciled us with the Father. What we do know about Jesus' suffering is that it did not change God. This also means it did not change Jesus. He was perfect and without sin before and after the Crucifixion. He did reparation for the damage done against the majesty of God the Father, but even this did not change God. This is not what the satisfaction made to God means.

God did this for our sake, meaning to change us for the better. The origin of sin in the Garden of Eden is when the serpent seduced Eve to distrust God. When the serpent said, "You will not die, God knows that the moment you eat of it you shall be as God," he is accusing God of deceiving the man and the woman. This is how the serpent enslaved them and their descendants to the fear of death. God gave them the way to eternal life. The serpent gave the woman a commentary on the Word of God. In this commentary, he accused God of being a deceiver. The woman conceived the lie, and from that time on the descendants of Adam and Eve have distrust and fear of God. Not a holy fear of the Lord, but just the opposite. When Jesus suffered and died, he was still innocent. He was made perfect by suffering in the sense that he proved that God cannot deceive nor can He be deceived. He reconciled us with God, not by changing the way God felt about us, but changing the way we feel about God. Now that it has been proven to humanity that God is all holy and perfect, and God cannot change, we are able to put our trust in God. We can put away all false gods and false ideas about the way to eternal life. There is only one way. Jesus is the way, the truth and the life. It is the Word of God that sustains life for all eternity, and Jesus is appointed to judge the living and the dead.

Jesus Predicts the End of the Drought

You have been reading about droughts, and droughts can last long enough to cause famines. The drought that Jesus promised to end is larger than anything we can imagine. This drought began when Adam and Eve were cast out of the Garden of Eden. The Jews were waiting for the Messiah. In reality, the whole Creation awaited the Savior. St. Paul explained this as the Creation being in labor. The bodies buried in the earth are like the seeds that could not grow until the Lord sent rain upon the earth. One of the last sayings of Jesus from the cross was, "I thirst." St. Teresa of Calcutta said Jesus thirsts for love and for souls. Only love can unite souls and hold them together as a body. Without love, souls would remain separate beings as the dust of the earth. As much as dust needs water to form clay, souls need love to form the body of Christ. St. Paul said that we are spiritual stones that make up the temple.

THE BODY

Jesus revealed that He would draw everyone to Himself. All would gather on Mount Calvary, even those who worship false gods, and those who eat at the table of Herodias. He indicated the kind of death He would die: *"And just as Moses lifted up the serpent in the desert, so must the Son of Man be lifted up, so that everyone who believes in him may have eternal life"* (John 3:14-15). *"And when I am lifted up from the earth, I will draw everyone to myself"* (John 12:32). He was lifted up from the earth on the cross. *"When Jesus saw his mother and the disciple there whom he loved, he said to his mother, 'Woman, behold your son.' Then he said to the disciple, 'Behold your mother.' And from that hour the disciple took her into his home"* (John 19:26-27). John at the foot of the cross represents all those who would become children of Mary. Jesus said, "Behold your son." The one she beheld with her eyes is her son, Jesus. When she conceived Jesus in her womb, she conceived what she heard. She conceived the Word of God. At the Crucifixion, she conceived in her Immaculate Heart the one she beheld with her eyes. She conceived the Image of God. I spoke about this in greater detail in the book, *The Hidden Life of Jesus*. The Sacred Heart of Jesus and the Immaculate Heart of Mary are united, and John took both into his home, because he took into his home the One he beheld with his eyes. He took the Ark of the Covenant into his home.

The Interior

Jesus died on the cross, and His soul went into the belly of the earth. He went to search for Adam to forgive his sin and Eve with him. When Jesus died, there was also an earthquake. The veil of the temple was torn from top to bottom, and graves were opened. When Jesus resurrected, many of the saints who had died rose from the open graves and appeared to people who knew them. Jesus ended the drought with His death and resurrection. He cannot die again, because he lives forever.

"On the evening of that first day of the week, when the doors were locked where the disciples were, for fear of the Jews, Jesus came and stood in their midst and said to them, 'Peace be with you.' When he had said this, he showed them his hands and his side. The disciples rejoiced when they saw the Lord. Jesus said to them again, 'Peace be with you. As the Father has sent me, so I send you.' And when he had said this, he breathed on them and said to them, 'Receive the Holy Spirit'" (John 20:19-22).

The disciples experienced death when Jesus died. Jesus is the head, and He was filled with the Holy Spirit. When Jesus died on the cross, the disciples were left without a soul. The first Adam was formed from the earth; but Jesus rose from the earth. He blew into the nostrils of His disciples the breath of life, and they became living beings. United as one Man, Jesus the High Priest. From this time on, all the functions of the priesthood are done standing in the person of Christ the High Priest. Essentially, Jesus raised his own body.

CHOICE—TO BELIEVE OR NOT TO BELIEVE

After Jesus said, "Receive the Holy Spirit," He added, "Whose sins you forgive are forgiven them, and whose sins you retain are retained." The Levite priests were the guardians of the Holy Sanctuary in the temple. I am not talking about the temple guards—that is different. What I mean about the priesthood is for the Jews to come back to the temple after they have become ritually unclean or are excommunicated by sin. They had to come back through the priesthood. There was no other way to return to the temple worship except through the priests. Whatever sacrifice was offered could only be offered to God by a priest.

Jesus instructed His disciples to guard the holy sanctuary of the church as the priests guarded the holy sanctuary of the temple. Those who want to reconcile with the church and repent will be forgiven. They must renounce the right to eat from the Tree of Knowledge of Good and Evil. They do so by renouncing Satan and all his empty promises, such as, "You shall not die, the moment you eat of it, you shall be as God." To be as God means that one cannot die. Those who renounce the right to eat from the Tree of Knowledge of Good and Evil by repenting, receives the privilege to eat from the Tree of Life (the Eucharist). It is a choice to believe or not to believe. Who are those that choose to believe? They are the faithful. Jesus used the encounter with Thomas as an example of those who must see to believe.

"*Thomas, called Didymus, one of the Twelve, was not with them when Jesus came. So the other disciples said to him, 'We* have seen the Lord.' But he said to them, 'Unless I see the mark of the nails in his hands and put my finger into the nailmarks and put my hand into his side, I will not believe.' Now a week later his disciples were again inside and Thomas was with them. Jesus came, although the doors were locked, and stood in their midst and said, 'Peace be with you.' Then he said to Thomas, 'Put your finger here and see my hands, and bring your hand and put it into my side, and do not be unbelieving, but believe.' Thomas answered and said to him, 'My Lord and my God!' Jesus said to him, 'Have you come to believe because you have seen me? Blessed are those who have not seen and have believed'" (John 20:24-29).

The soul and thoughts are both spiritual and invisible. In the unity prayer, soul and thoughts unite body and head.

Head (physical)	Lips Eyes Ears	Visible
Spiritual	Thoughts Souls	Invisible
Body (physical)	Hearts Hands Feet	Visible

Chapter Four

Twelve Apostles—Firstborn of Jesus

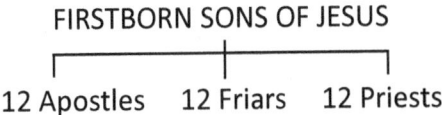

THE LORD GOD PUT HIS plan of salvation to work through His firstborn. It was in phases: beginning with Adam, then Israel and climaxing with his only begotten Son, Jesus Christ. All three were called the firstborn Son of God, but Jesus is the only begotten Son of God.

Pentecost begins a new era, when Jesus works through His firstborn sons. The twelve apostles are the firstborn of the New Israel, with Peter being the prince of the apostles. The promise that God would make His dwelling with humanity has come into fulfillment. Pentecost is the beginning of the earth being set on fire. The second chapter of the Book of Acts has the conversion of Jews and converts to Judaism from every nation under heaven. About three thousand persons accepted baptism and were added that day. In the fourth chapter in the Book of Acts, the number of believers increased to about five thousand men. The tenth chapter has the conversion of Cornelius the Centurion and his household. The church is now one, Jews and Gentiles alike. The Greek-speaking Jews at Pentecost, Hebrew in the temple, when the man was healed at the beautiful gate, and the Latin Cornelius and his household—all three experiences happened after St. Peter spoke to them. This is important to understand, because the Pope is the sign of unity for the Church. It is also important for the *Flame of Love* movement, which is the new Pentecost, to note that the Flame of Love is spread by speech. It is a new era where all Christians become missionaries, sent out to the missions two-by-two. Each person is sent out as a missionary, with Jesus as partner. That is what He asks of us, and to affirm this we are asked to pray for this in the prayer He gave to Elizabeth Kindelmann, *The Unity Prayer*. May our feet journey together, may our hands gather in unity.

Head
Falling into Ruin

So, if the earth was set on fire at Pentecost, why is the *Flame of Love of the Immaculate Heart of Mary* necessary? The one hundred and twenty in the upper room were formed from the earth. The Holy Spirit gave life to the newborn Church. Each member has the indwelling of the Trinity for interior life, and the fire rested on their heads. The Church is a new creation. Like the first Creation, in order for the life of the Church to be sustained, the Word of God must be obeyed. Jesus promised that the gates of hell shall not prevail over His Church, and it has not. However, the Church is in danger, and it will be under attack until the end of time.

The first period of the Church seemed like a drought, because there were many martyrs for the faith. These prophets were willing to suffer and die, rather than abandon the truth. We believe that the blood of the martyrs is seed for the Church. So long as Christianity was not legal in the Roman Empire, the Church remained underground, as a seed planted in the ground. Jesus' thirst for love was not quenched. The Christians were waiting for rain, and it appeared that the drought ended only when Constantine, according to his biographer, Eusebius, had this experience: *"He saw with his own eyes the trophy of a cross of light in the heavens, above the sun, and bearing the inscription, CONQUER BY THIS. At this sight he himself was struck with amazement, and his whole army also, which followed him on this expedition, and witnessed the miracle."* With the Edict of Milan came the end of legalized segregation. The Church would rise from underground and blossom.

It did not take long before problems arose from within. The Church began to suffer from the same ailments that the Israelites suffered from: false prophets. Beginning with Arius, there appeared a cycle of prophets, all of them priests, who strived to define Jesus' humanity, divinity, will, and nature, His relationship with His mother, with the Father and the Holy Spirit. The only problem with searching for truth is when legitimate authority is rejected. Anyone who goes up against the devil alone will suffer the fate of Adam and Eve. He will first be deceived as Eve was, and if he persists in obstinacy he will be cast out.

The choice is always with acceptance or rejection of the head. For the universal church the head is whoever sits on the chair of Peter. The bishop of Rome is not accepted as pastor by all Christians. Pope Leo I (Leo the Great) is responsible for a dogmatic epistle in 446 A. D. that proclaimed the Holy Spirit proceeds from both Father and Son. The idea that the Holy Spirit proceeds from the Father and the Son was not a problem until the Bishop of Rome declared it a truth, and it would be inserted into the Creed. The Council Fathers said that nothing could be added to the Creed. Here we begin to see a struggle for authority, between the Pope and College of Bishops. Who has the higher authority? Centuries later in the West, a name was given to the idea that a council had more authority than a Pope. It was called counciliarism. The first major schism occurred in 451 A.D., although the cause was not attributed to the Filioque; the authority of Pope Leo I was rejected.

INTERIOR

The schism between East and West was made complete in 1054 A.D. The Filioque was included in the reasons, but the main objection of the churches in the East was that the Latin church used unleavened bread for the Eucharist. Their objection to using unleavened bread was that Jesus had already been resurrected, so the Latin church should not use unleavened bread. It is after the Greek Orthodox and Roman Catholic schism that Jesus requested to St. Francis of Assisi to go and repair His church, which was falling into ruin. He did not say *has fallen* as in the case of Adam and Eve. Adam and Eve's story is about fallen humanity or the Fall.

In the Latin church, Christians continue to separate themselves from the Bishop of Rome. The house continues to fall into ruin when Martin Luther definitively breaks with the church in 1522 A.D. I attribute the schism to that year, because he published his translation of the New Testament without permission or approval from the church. That appears to be his answer to being excommunicated, which was a call to repentance. What Luther said about the Eucharist is that the bread and wine does not become the body and blood of Jesus during the consecration. Summed up it means that he does not believe that the Man becomes a living being when the breath of life is breathed on him by the priest. He joined the Orthodox in that he also does not see the Resurrection in the Consecration.

Body

Finally, man wants to return to the ground from which he was taken. King Henry VIII wanted to live on through his offspring. He wanted a son, through sexual reproduction, who would ascend the throne as king. Reproduction is the basic means of salvation for humans, as with all species of life. It preserves us from extinction, but a religious liturgy is more lending to eternal salvation. Henry VIII did not change the Liturgy. His interest was marriage and reproduction. In natural reproduction, the man returns to the ground when the sperm enters the egg. The man, given the title "Defender of the Faith," did not believe he would have a son. Did he lose his voice as Adam and Zechariah did? Maybe Henry would have had a son named John had he not hardened his heart and put away his wife.

CHOICE TO BELIEVE OR NOT BELIEVE

When King Henry VIII divorced Catherine of Aragon, it was a divorce with Spain. He could have had a son named John, if he had remained Defender of the Faith. He would have been Defender of the Faith in the New World. This way, as king, he could have been a father to a son named John (Juan Diego). Since he had to see in order to believe, he was deprived of the blessing he could not see. What I mean by this is that the blessing of the fruit of the womb are children we can see. Spiritual children are not necessarily visible, and that is what Juan Diego was.

Chapter Five

Twelve Franciscan Friars— Firstborn of Jesus

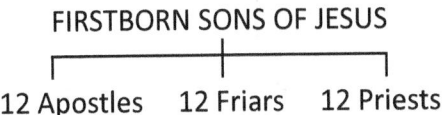

WERE THE FRANCISCANS CALLED TO repair the Church alone? The answer is, *no!* But they are the firstborn of Jesus among a new form of religious order. Up until this time in history, monasticism was responsible in large part for the conversion of Europe, and the spread of Christianity in the world. The great monastic orders will never lose their importance in this battle for souls. However, something was different during this time in salvation history from the time that the Church was converting pagans. The difference is that Christians had become segregated. The Church was falling into ruin, because the divisions among Christians became the destruction of Jesus' body (the temple). So, we have a new problem, and Jesus has a new solution.

Jesus' answer to this falling away from communion with Rome was to send missionaries out to the people—thus, the beginning of the mendicant orders. They would go out and work for their sustenance, and if that failed, they would beg as Elijah did, renouncing themselves and giving up everything.

I would like to reflect on the four major mendicant orders, and their relationship to the *Flame of Love of the Immaculate Heart of Mary*. These orders served the needs of the Church in the battle against heresies, beginning with the Albigenses. The mendicants were also effective in evangelization. Each group contributed with their charisms and met the needs of the Church with their gifts. You may wonder why I recognize the Franciscans as Jesus' firstborn. Actually, they are all part of a whole, but the Franciscans reflect the first step in the creation of man.

The Body

God formed the man from the clay of the earth. This is first in the Creation story, and it is first in repairing Jesus' house. Jesus spoke to St. Francis from the Crucifix in the Chapel of St. Damien saying, "Francis, go and repair my house, which is falling into ruin." Francis repaired the rundown and neglected little church. After doing so, he repaired St. Peter's and St. Mary of the Angels chapels also. His approach was much like Elijah: he went out begging for stones. He repaired the chapels as Elijah repaired the altar. Because St. Francis was faithful in small matters, he was entrusted with greater responsibility. He made friends with dishonest wealth and was trusted with true wealth. The dishonest wealth was money, because the dishonest judge uses it to enslave people. He gained it by deceit and those who serve money cannot serve God. Of course, I am speaking of the devil, who gained dominion of the earth by deceit. The chapels are important, but repairing the chapels are a small matter compared to the salvation of souls. Repairing Jesus' house with spiritual stones (souls) is a greater responsibility, because the souls are the true wealth. Like Elijah, Francis was commissioned to bring the Israelites back to their senses, to lead them back to the Church where the sacrifice was offered by the priesthood of Christ. The twelve friars were the first of the four mendicant orders to receive approval of their rule from the Pope. To evangelize and bring the spiritual stones needed to build the body of Christ is the first phase of reparation. Jesus gave St. Francis the stigmata. He became an image of the Crucified Christ, who from the cross said, "I thirst," and drew everyone to Himself. The work of the body in missionary work is expressed in the desires of Jesus: "May our feet journey together, may our hands gather in unity." The Franciscans went out in pairs, two-by-two, to preach and minister to the needs of the people. We are privileged individually to journey with Jesus, and gather with Jesus.

The Interior

God blew into his nostrils the breath of life, and so man became a living being. The Carmelite Order, whose focus is the interior life, were given what is needed for evangelization in that respect. Interestingly, these groups were blessed with private revelations and given something that would bless Christians in this life, and eternity. If the heart and soul represents the interior life of the person, then the brown scapular is the work garment that keeps the baptismal gown clean. The Blessed Virgin Mary gave the scapular to St. Simon Stock, along with promises for those who wear it. Most importantly is the promise that we will be raised back to life as the widow's son, when the breath of life returned to his body.

Let me use this opportunity to reiterate: the books of St. John of the Cross, *The Assent to Carmel* and *The Dark Night*, are a must-read for anyone interested in Carmelite spirituality. *The Flame of Love of the Immaculate Heart of Mary* went forth from the Carmel. This is the story of Elijah and the widow, the spiritual and the sensual. May our hearts beat in unison; may our souls be in harmony. Jesus is the musician; we are the instruments.

The Head

Everyone who receives the gift of the *Flame of Love of the Immaculate Heart of Mary* becomes a living being of a new kind; an individual whose heart and soul are impregnated with Jesus. We must add our own love to this fire until it blazes into a flame which cannot be contained. That is the time of labor, when we give birth to Jesus. However, to become a living being is not enough. Our lives must be sustained by the Word of God. He is the way to eternal life; the truth.

To bring back the heretics during the time of St. Dominic, the Blessed Virgin Mary gave him the rosary. Before this he preached the truth to them, yet with little success. Once he began to pray the rosary, there was another power behind his preaching, and the evangelization was considerably more successful. Obedience to the Word of God is a choice to believe or not to believe. The interpretation of the Word of God must always be viewed through the lens of the literal sense. This will keep us from being deceived by a spiritual interpretation that contradicts the literal sense. The spiritual sense will never say that the literal sense is a lie. This is what the devil told Eve when he said, "Surely you will not die." God said they would die if they ate the forbidden fruit, so how could the devil's commentary say that God did not mean what He said? The Dominicans were sent to preach the truth in order to bring the Christians back to their senses and renounce the empty promises of Satan. Their preaching was to give the people the thoughts that God wanted conveyed. This would silence the chaotic voices of all the false prophets; the confused languages of Babylon. May our thoughts be as one; may our ears listen to the silence together.

THE FACE

The fourth major mendicant order are the Augustinians. Their spirituality is searching for God. Up to this point I have not mentioned the face. The creation was body, interior, and head. Once our first parents sinned, they were ashamed and did not want to face God. *"And when they heard the voice of the Lord God walking in Paradise at the afternoon air, Adam and his wife hid themselves from the face of the Lord God, amidst the* trees of Paradise. And the Lord God called Adam, and said to him, 'Where art thou?' and he said, 'I heard thy voice in Paradise; and I was afraid, because I was naked, and I hid myself.'"(Gen. 3:8-10) From that incident, it is believed that no one looks on the face of God and lives. Presumably, this means no one guilty of sin may look on the face of God.

The founders of the four major mendicant orders all received a gift from Jesus or Mary through private revelation. Jesus gave the stigmata to St. Francis. The Blessed Virgin Mary gave the Brown Scapular to St. Simon Stock, although he is more of a proxy, since the Carmelites do not have a founder. The Blessed Virgin Mary gave the rosary to St. Dominic. God gave a voice to St. Augustine, the voice of a child. Here is a section from St. Augustine's Diary that reveals his search for God:

Confessions of St. Augustine:
Chapter 12 – The Voice in the Garden

I cast myself down I know not how, under a certain fig-tree, giving full vent to my tears; and the floods of mine eyes gushed out an acceptable sacrifice to Thee (Ps 51:19). And, not indeed in these words, yet to this purpose, spake I much unto Thee: and Thou, O Lord, how long? (Ps 6:4) how long, Lord, wilt Thou be angry for ever? (Ps 79:5, 8) Remember not our former iniquities, for I felt that I was held by them. I sent up these sorrowful words: How long, how long, "to-morrow, and tomorrow?" Why not now? why not is there this hour an end to my uncleanness?

So was I speaking and weeping in the most bitter contrition of my heart, when, lo! I heard from a neighbouring house a voice, as of boy or girl, I know not, chanting, and oft repeating, "Take up and read; Take up and read." Instantly, my countenance altered, I began to think most intently whether children were wont in any kind of play to sing such words: nor could I remember ever to have heard the like. So checking the torrent of my tears, I arose; interpreting it to be no other than a command from God to open the book, and read the first chapter I should find. For I had heard of Antony, that coming in during the reading of the Gospel, he received the admonition, as if what was being read was spoken to him: Go, sell all that thou hast, and give to the poor, and thou shalt have treasure in heaven, and come and follow me: (Mt 19:21) *and by such oracle he was forthwith converted unto Thee. Eagerly then I returned to the place where Alypius was sitting; for there had I laid the volume of the Apostle when I arose thence. I seized, opened, and in silence read that section on which my eyes first fell: Not in rioting and drunkenness, not in chambering and wantonness, not in strife and envying; but put ye on the Lord Jesus Christ, and make not provision for the flesh, in concupiscence* (Rom 13:13-14). *No further would I read; nor needed I: for instantly at the end of this sentence, by a light as it were of serenity infused into my heart, all the darkness of doubt vanished away.* (Saint Augustine, *The Confessions of St. Augustine,* (pp. 125-126) Kindle Edition).

Although St. Augustine lived about eight centuries before the Hermits of St. Augustine formed into a mendicant order, they accepted the Rule of St. Augustine, as did the Dominicans. There is an even longer period from St. Augustine to Elizabeth Kindelmann, yet the similarity is undeniable. He heard the voice, and because of his deep repentance he was not afraid to look into the eyes of God. He was ready to be judged, and he encountered the face of the Lord God in the Sacred Scriptures.

The charism of the Order of St. Augustine has three parts: spirituality (searching for God – during prayer Augustine found himself, God, and his brothers); fraternity (community life – the Augustinians encounter God through fraternity; peace and harmony among the brothers is a sign from the Holy Spirit that is dwelling within the Augustinians and constitutes a testimony to the whole Church, "Be of one mind and heart"); and ministry (service to the Church – the Augustinians make themselves available to the Church to announce and live the reign of God).

As I said earlier, "We have a new problem, and Jesus has a new solution." We are to search for God instead of hiding from Him. The idea is to become one with God. Adoration is a means of experiencing an encounter with God, and we can save souls even in the quiet of the night when alone with Jesus. These were the words of Jesus to Elizabeth Kindelmann. We are called to adore Jesus and be intercessors. May our glances profoundly penetrate each other, and may our lips pray together to gain mercy from the Eternal Father.

Chapter Six

The Twelve Priests of Hungary—Firstborn of Jesus

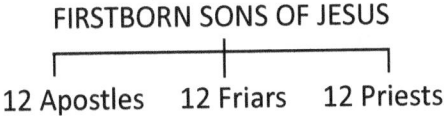

JESUS TOLD ELIZABETH KINDELMANN THAT He chose twelve of the best priests in Hungary. They would help her take the *Flame of Love* of His Mother's heart from Hungary to the rest of the world. Before this happened, Jesus told Elizabeth she must fast and pray for the twelve priests. The process of gaining the priests for this mission was anything but quick and easy. Sometime between March 4 and March 7 of 1962, Jesus asked Elizabeth to fast and pray for the twelve priests for twelve weeks. However, she was to continue to fast and pray for them. A year later, the Blessed Virgin gave Elizabeth some hope of accomplishing their goal but without indicating a specific time. She said to Elizabeth, "We have no time to lose. A definite time is determined before my Flame of Love will ignite, exactly the time Satan needs to test the excellent twelve chosen priestly souls." This was during March of 1963. Elizabeth continued to fast and pray for the priests. Jesus came to her with great news around November 13, 1964 and said, *"...Be at peace, My little one. I have irradiated such a great light in the soul of your confessor, that by its brightness he sees clearly the road he must follow to put into action our Holy Cause... We have gained one of the twelve."* (*The Spiritual Diary*—page 233)

It took two years and eight months before one of the priests had been enlightened. We should not lose hope when we do not see the results that we expect; this is proof that we must put our total trust in Jesus, as Elizabeth was asked to do.

THE DROUGHT

Let's go back to how the *Flame of Love* was introduced to Elizabeth Kindelmann. The twelve priests would take the cause to the rest of the world from their twelve churches, but this would take years. It all began with a drought. Elizabeth suffered for about three years what St. John of the Cross called "the dark night." This dryness in her spiritual life would prepare her for the mission for which she was created. The drought appears to end in death, but it actually ends with birth. When Elijah came to the widow of Zarephath, she was prepared to eat the last meal and die. Jesus—after three hours of darkness on the cross, right before his death—said, "My God, my God, why have you abandoned me?" Elizabeth Kindelmann at the end of this dark night said, "God doesn't want to have anything to do with me." She was deprived of consolations during this drought. Somehow, God uses this to prepare the soil for producing abundant fruit. Jesus would flood her soul with abundant graces, but He had to make room for these graces first.

THE BODY

At the end of the drought, Jesus came to Elizabeth with the request to renounce herself. To renounce herself completely, she would have to put her total trust in Jesus. *The Flame of Love must begin at Carmel, as the widow who put her total trust in Elijah. She gave her last and her all by first baking a little cake for Elijah.* Elizabeth Kindelmann would give up everything, and separate herself from the world, in as much as a contemplative nun does. She is the widow with her son that Jesus would draw to himself by asking her to take care of his needs. *The Blessed Virgin Mary spoke to Elizabeth for the first time saying, "My dear little Carmelite!"* Elizabeth said, *"When I heard her voice, a great river of repentance flooded my soul. When I heard this sweet voice two more times, tears of sorrow for my sins flowed out. Mary: Then the Blessed Mother said, "Adore my Divine Son and make reparation." (Spiritual Diary – page 10)*. In these conversations, Jesus and Mary revealed how all the surface of the earth would be watered before the Lord formed the first man. Here are three examples Jesus used, which explain a stream watering all the face of the earth: *(1.) "Pass My words on to those concerned and plead with them not to impede this great river of grace which My Mother, through her Flame of Love, wants to run over the earth." (2.) "The current of My graces, powerful like an overflowing river, would act in your souls in an uninterrupted way and with a constant intensity, if your repentance, like a powerful river, was rushing toward Me and surrendering to Me!" (3.) "The water of My graces, like a stream, flows continually into your soul. Now is the moment to tell you why these abundant graces remain in your soul. By your sacrifices, you have dug a deep channel and the water of My Divine Graces, with its purifying power, has found a place in your soul. If you had not prepared this deep channel by your sacrifices, the purifying water of My graces would have drained off."* (Spiritual Diary – pp 161, 267, 234). Of course, these examples will only sound sensible to someone who sees the house being built from the ground up, with Elizabeth being the earth.

Jesus will draw those to himself who receive the *Flame of Love of the Immaculate Heart of Mary.* Many will become children of Mary, and those who were already children of Mary will begin to share in her Immaculate Conception. As the *Flame of Love* spreads throughout the world, the Lord is forming his body from the clay of the earth. We are united by love. It is love that makes us one body, and repentance allows us to experience love.

The reparation that is being done by the *Flame of Love* is done by repairing the house from the ground up. It starts with the earth, and from the earth the man is formed. The man is formed from her, as much as John the Baptist was formed in the womb of his mother Elizabeth. Jesus filled him with the Holy Spirit, the breath of life, and the infant John became a living being. He became a living being because he was set free from the original sin. Those who were drawn together at first were Elizabeth's family. Jesus wanted to save her parish, and their country, Hungary. In the meantime, she was encouraged to take the cause to her spiritual director, then the Bishop, and ultimately to the Pope. The house is being repaired from the ground up. The work of the body of missionaries is that our feet journey together; and may our hands gather in unity.

INTERIOR

The interior life of the body, in this era, is the *Flame of Love of the Immaculate Heart of Mary*. As the *Flame of Love* spreads, the Church will become more alive because she will experience new birth. This new birth is the new evangelization. We are praying that the effect of grace will spread over all of humanity. All the hearts will be enlightened, because Jesus will dwell in the hearts of his disciples. *The Flame of Love*, as the Blessed Virgin said, will arrive in this way: "As a soft light, it will arouse no suspicions. This is the miracle that will come forth from your hearts." (*Spiritual Diary* – page 39). *The Flame of Love* is the interior life of man, which began at the Carmel. It will make the whole Church missionary by making the whole Church contemplative. May our hearts beat in unison; may our souls be in harmony.

THE HEAD

The movement is meant to spread throughout the world, to repair the Church from the ground up. Ultimately the *Flame of Love* must receive more than apostolic blessings from the popes. It must eventually become the blessing that was given to the first man and woman: *"Be fertile and multiply; fill the earth and subdue it"* (Genesis 1:28). When this happens, the world will eat from all the fruit trees in the garden that are good for food. Jesus will reign in the hearts of the faithful and the Word of God will sustain the life of those who believe. The choice is to believe or not to believe. As Jesus told Elizabeth Kindelmann, *"Renounce yourself, I do not force you. You have your free will. I have many graces to give you, but you cannot receive them unless you renounce yourself."* (*Spiritual Diary* – page 7) Elizabeth Kindelmann is the mother of this great religious order. She suffered great labor pains for us to receive these gifts. Repair of the house must continue upwards until it reaches the holy father, the Vicar of Christ. May our thoughts be as one; may our ears listen to the silence together.

THE FACE

Elizabeth was kneeling before the tabernacle in the chapel dedicated to the Holy Spirit. The Lord Jesus said to her, *"Look into My eyes! I allow our eyes to look at one another and our gazes to be as one. Do not see anything else. Read in My tearful eyes that I rest on you the anxious desire of My love. Make reparation! This is the only consolation you can give Me. I, the Man-God eager for your hearts, I need your consolation."* (*Spiritual Diary* – page 207)

This appears as something new in salvation history, that we are to look on the face of God. After Adam and Eve disobeyed God, they hid from God. As mentioned in Chapter Five, when the Lord called out to the man, "Where are you?" The man said, "I heard you in the garden, but I was afraid, because I was naked, so I hid myself." This literally means, *I heard your voice, so I hid from your face.* The man was afraid of being judged. In these last days, we have received an outpouring of grace, and nothing like this has happened since the Word became flesh. *The Flame of Love of the Immaculate Heart of Mary* allows us to save souls even while adoring Jesus in the quiet of the night. We can look into Jesus' eyes, and save souls by interceding for them. May our glances profoundly penetrate each other, and may our lips pray together to gain mercy from the Eternal Father.

ACTIVE	CONTEMPLATIVE
1. May our feet journey together	8. May our lips pray together to gain mercy from the Eternal Father
2. May our hands gather in unity	7. May our glances profoundly penetrate each other
3. May our hearts beat in unison	6. May our ears listen to the silence together
4. May our souls be in harmony	5. May our thoughts be as one

Summary

THE FOUR MAJOR MENDICANT ORDERS each with its own charisms and missionary function are:

1: Franciscans—The Body

2: Carmelites—The Interior

3: Dominicans—The Head

4: Augustinians—The Face

One priest left the Augustinians and formed his theology, it appears, based on the fear of death. The fear of eternal separation from God overwhelmed him, and instead of searching for God, he began to search for consolation and certitude. That priest is Martin Luther. One priest caused the spark that led to the Protestant Reformation. This is no reflection on the Augustinian Order. They have remained faithful to the mission of saving souls, and the Church has benefited from their charisms throughout the centuries.

Luther left the Augustinians and led many into segregation as denominations in Reformed Christianity. This was done by the leadership (or should I say *actions*) of one man, who misunderstood two things: Divine Mercy and Purgatory. The descendants of the Reformation fathers do not understand Divine Mercy as the Catholic Church teaches, and they are not taught to pray for the souls in Purgatory, since they do not believe Purgatory exists.

THE MARIAN FATHERS OF THE IMMACULATE CONCEPTION OF THE BLESSED VIRGIN MARY

The reverse of this story is a religious order founded in 1673 in Poland. This group struggled for survival under different circumstances in history. It was finally oppressed by Czarist Russia, and only one member remained in the order by 1908. Two priests joined this single priest and the order was revived. Today, the order is known as the Marian Fathers of the Immaculate Conception of the Blessed Virgin Mary. Their main charisms are promoting Divine Mercy, and offering prayers and reparation for the souls in Purgatory. The Church had a new problem, and Jesus offered a new solution.

The Marian Fathers also seem to have a very profound understanding of Scripture and history. The Sacred Heart of Jesus and the Immaculate Heart of Mary are examples of where their profound insights and understanding have benefitted the Church, promoting consecration to the Sacred Heart of Jesus and the Immaculate Heart of Mary. It appears they are one of two orders that see Scripture more as the early Church did.

The Marian Fathers explain popular devotion with in-depth understanding.

MISSIONARIES OF CHARITY

The Missionaries of Charity, founded by St. Teresa of Calcutta, are another group that has a profound impact on evangelization. Their charism is different from the Marian Fathers, in the sense that the Marian Fathers are promoting what they understand. They are helping the Church to revive in areas that promote evangelization from within. The Missionaries of Charity are different, because of Mother Teresa. She revealed insights that we do not hear others speak of in the way that she does. She shares the understanding of the early Church. I wonder if this could be the order that Benedict XVI wrote about in the book, *The Theology of St. Bonaventure in History*. He wrote this thesis before he became a bishop. He spoke of a new order in the last days that would be like a combination of Francis and Dominic. This also means like John and Paul. I do not know if this relates to the Missionaries of Charity or the Marian Fathers of the Immaculate Conception of the Blessed Virgin Mary. *It could even be the Flame of Love of the Immaculate Heart of Mary*. God Knows!

Mother Teresa explained the *Flame of Love of the Immaculate Heart of Mary* without even referring to it. Let's look at her teachings.

The four major mendicant orders each with its own charisms and missionary functions are:

MENDICANTS	REPAIR THE CHURCH	GIFTS FROM JESUS AND MARY	TEACHINGS OF ST. TERESA OF CALCUTTA	THE FLAME OF LOVE
Franciscans	The Body	The Stigmata	I Thirst – Jesus on the cross	1. May our feet journey together 2. May our hands gather in unity
Carmelites	The Interior	The Brown Scapular	Mother, lend me your heart, and I will give you my heart	3. May our hearts beat in unison 4. May our souls be in harmony
Dominicans	The Head	The Rosary	To give your word, is to give yourself	5. May our thoughts be as one 6. May our ears listen to the silence together
Augustinian	The Face	Locution	Look into Jesus' penetrating eyes on the cross, and see into his heart	7. May our glances profoundly penetrate each other 8. May our lips pray together to gain mercy from the Eternal Father

St. Teresa of Calcutta also taught that the religious in her order (men, women, active, contemplative, and priest) are based on the five wounds of Christ Crucified.

1. *We kiss the wound of your sacred left hand with sorrow deep and true.*
2. *We kiss the wound of your sacred right hand with sorrow deep and true.*
3. *We kiss the wound of your sacred left foot with sorrow deep and true.*
4. *We kiss the wound of your sacred right foot with sorrow deep and true.*
5. *We kiss the wound of your sacred side with sorrow deep and true.*

www.ingramcontent.com/pod-product-compliance
Lightning Source LLC
Chambersburg PA
CBHW050446010526
44118CB00013B/1702